HouseBeautiful

500 BATHROOM IDEAS

HouseBeautiful
500 BATHROOM IDEAS
ELEGANT & DREAMY SPACES

Barbara King

HEARST BOOKS

New York

HEARST BOOKS
New York

An Imprint of Sterling Publishing
387 Park Avenue South
New York, NY 10016

ISBN 978-1-58816-983-9

Distributed in Canada by Sterling Publishing
c/o Canadian Manda Group, 165 Dufferin Street
Toronto, Ontario, Canada M6K 3H6

Distributed in the United Kingdom by GMC Distribution Services
Castle Place, 166 High Street, Lewes, East Sussex, England BN7 1XU

Distributed in Australia by Capricorn Link (Australia) Pty. Ltd.
P.O. Box 704, Windsor, NSW 2756, Australia

For information about custom editions, special sales, and premium and corporate purchases,
please contact Sterling Special Sales at 800-805-5489 or specialsales@sterlingpublishing.com.

Printed in China

2 4 6 8 10 9 7 5 3 1

www.sterlingpublishing.com

HouseBeautiful
500 BATHROOM IDEAS

A special thanks to the editors of House Beautiful, in particular

Kitchen and Bath Editor Samantha Emmerling and Interiors Editor Doretta Sperduto,

and the photography stylists who helped bring these rooms to life.

Contents

Chapter 1 Luxurious

17

26

32

40

42

44

48

51

54

57

58

63

65

70

75

"A GREAT BATHROOM IS MADE UP OF GREAT DETAILS. IT'S LIKE A PORSCHE SPEEDSTER OR AN HERMES KELLY BAG—FOREVER ELEGANT AND TIMELESS."

—CHAD EISNER

1

A master bath conjures images of a grand European salon with its Roman tub—carved from a single block of marble—blue marble walls, and rug-like floor, trimmed in mosaic tile.

2

An oversize antique French ceiling
fixture and theatrical, ceiling-high
linen curtains are compelling enough
to lead your eye through the room to
the French doors and out to the garden.

3

Subtle gradations of neutral colors
inspire calm.

4

Bathrooms that feel like rooms rather than just a place to bathe inspire nestling. This is an homage to the ceremonial bath, where you relax and contemplate simple pleasures.

5

A George III–style secretary bookcase takes the place of a built-in vanity. Café curtains on lower windows provide privacy but allow light to spill in.

6

Irresistibly lady-like, a cluster of pearls, a dresser jar, and perfume bottles on an antique tray glimmer on the secretary/vanity.

7

A nineteenth-century English secretary takes center stage, introducing a grace note of formality and a thoroughly surprising focal point. ◀

8

A mirrored wall creates the illusion of stepping into another, identical room—one that's fully furnished. An antique commode was refitted with a limestone sink.

9

Sandblasted glass walls sheltering the toilet and shower, a vanity designed to look like furniture, and a mirror in an elaborate gilded frame make this space feel like a real room. The honed veined marble floor rectangles are set in a running bond to keep the space from looking too formal. ◄

10

Flaunting its curves, a voluptuous bathroom says, "Indulge yourself." The arched window repeats its shape in the top shelves.

11

The tub, big enough for two, has wonderfully comfortable neck rests on each side. A flatscreen TV looks surprisingly at home on a bottom shelf.

12

The arch is repeated again in the white lacquer mirror and deco-inspired vanity. Handblown glass sconces have a machine-age shape and give off a milky glow, perfect for a romantic nighttime bath. The 1940s ceiling light is made of Murano glass petals with gold flecks that twinkle.

13

Bath fittings straddle the line between modern and vintage. They're satin nickel, which has a hand-rubbed appearance.

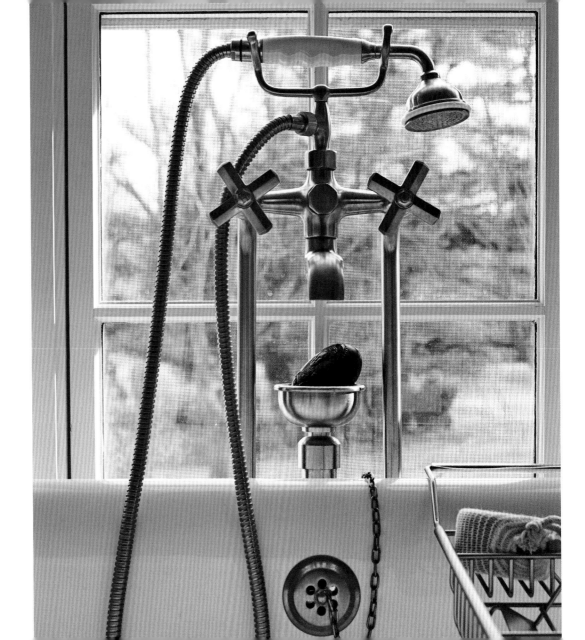

14

Mercury glass and silver-gilt accessories add elegant shimmer to the vanity, and a footed dish varies the scale. ▶

15

The honed gray limestone floor tiles are laid in a chevron pattern to add movement. Softer than marble, it's almost like having a rug underfoot.

16

This room strikes a beautiful balance between feminine and masculine. Crystal teardrops on the sconces and cut-glass knobs on the glass door of the marble-lined shower throw off even more sparkle.

17

A generous mirror opposite a window in the shower bounces light around and doubles the sparkling beauty of an antique crystal chandelier.

18

The tub is an adaptation of styles popular in England and France in the late nineteenth century. The Louis Ghost chair references the history in a playful way.

19

It's crisp, clean, and efficient, with loads of marble and polished nickel, like a bathroom in a luxury hotel.

20

To increase the sense of space and openness, a double vanity without cabinets beneath was chosen. To compensate, the twin medicine cabinets are four inches deep—and the bonus is you don't have to crouch down.

21

A marbled tub niche exudes a stately classicism worthy of a Roman emperor. With a marble this elaborately veined, paying attention to the placement of the veining is important in order to show off the full beauty of the stone.

22

A glass insert in the door calls to mind the timeless appeal of an arched window. ▲

23

In only 42 square feet, it's a mini version of a fine hotel bath. The bumped-out wall is faced with Jerusalem Gold limestone, cut into 8-by-12-inch rectangles to echo the shape of the tub.

24

The wall's depth allows room for the niches, which are functional as well as decorative. The faucet stands on its own, leaving the limestone without the clutter of handles and a spout.

25

A matching vessel sink is set off by a stain-proof CaesarStone counter. The faucet matches the tub's and provides the right height for the sink. If the spout is too high, water splashes, and if it's too low, there's scant room for washing your hands. A light under the vanity highlights the open space underneath.

26

The toilet has an elongated seat but a slim tank, so it takes up less space. A mirror becomes a virtual second window.

27

Lustrous and lavish, a master bath is dressed like the powder room of a 1920s European hotel. A vanity table links a pair of mirrored bureaus—formerly in a bedroom—fitted with sinks.

28

A gilded mirror above adds even more glamour. The sconces have crystal arms, and the faucets have crystal handles that reflect ambient light at night.

30

A mirrored vanity tray is filled with perfumes and roses. Like the crystal accents, the gilt and mirror are light-reflective.

29

Calacatta marble enshrouding the tub completes the sumptuous look. Ornate gilt-and-crystal sconces add curves and age, and complement the hints of gold in the marble.

32

A finely carved 1930s French settee strikes a lady-like pose against the window.

31

Tile mosaics break up the expanse of marble on the floor. They're based on tile floors in a Parisian museum, but executed in a fresh modern way, like built-in rugs.

33

When it comes to indulging guests, not much tops a bathroom that has the grandness of a palace hotel in Paris. Gleaming silver tones enhance the old-world elegance.

34

An antique mirror propped behind the burnished French-style tub reflects a vintage pharmacy cabinet, which stores items best left hidden.

35

The abundance of Carrara marble and the eleven-foot-high ceilings were inspired by bathrooms in five-star hotels, such as the Plaza Athenee, the Ritz, George V, and the Crillon. Monsieur and Madame "mats" are inlaid mosaics. ◄

36

Open washstands make perfect sense for guests. Toiletries are readily accessible and also in plain sight, so they're less likely to be left behind. ▶

37

Silver napkin rings engraved with "Monsieur" and "Madame" sparked the idea for the tile mosaics in front of the sinks, including their shapely lettering. Inspiration is all around you!

38

A thermostatic control valve with porcelain accents gives a period feel to the ample shower.

39

A soaking tub was rimmed with marble, inspired by a tub in a stately hotel in Rome. The elegant porcelain console sinks capture Belle Epoque style. ◀

40

A flirtatious, flouncy skirt gives a couture billow to the sink in a woman's bathroom. The smoky gray-and-white stripes coordinate with the gray-and-white marble lining the wall. An antique French repoussé mirror flanked by delicate sconces injects a little glitz.

41

A mirrored vanity and tufted chaise have an old-Hollywood glamour reminiscent of a starlet's boudoir. The glass-front cabinet stacked with plush white towels contributes further to the more-than-just-a-bathroom impression.

42

Mirrored drawers in a vanity and a large three-panel mirror on the wall romanticize and expand the bathroom. Carrara marble is extended from the floor and up the tub.

43

The fabric on the Roman shades is dotted with sequins that catch even more light. The resin bowl chandelier is pierced resin, adding a modernized lacy note.

44

Flanked by simple matching vanities with bracket feet, a showstopping 1950s French mirrored armoire glamorizes and ages a master bath.

45

Squares of Ming green and bands of Chinese statuary marble mimic the look of paneling. The bathtub was floated in the middle of the room, with the glass shower bisecting its edge to create a shower seat. ◄

46

A stunning wall of blue and
white marble, cut by a water
jet into a delicate Art Nouveau-
like design called Danse Azul
by Artistic Tile, is the focal
point of this master bathroom.
The tub is encased in Calacatta
marble, which runs up the wall
above the faucets.

47

Soft baby-blue marble tile coordinates with the tub wall and sets off walnut cabinetry that looks like furniture, not built-ins.

48

Marble on these walls evokes sky and clouds, and the marble mosaic on the floor mimics a rug. A beveled mirror expands the perception of space. ▶

49

Even better than cushioned seating in a bay window is a luxe tub. Chinoiserie wallpaper dresses up the walls.

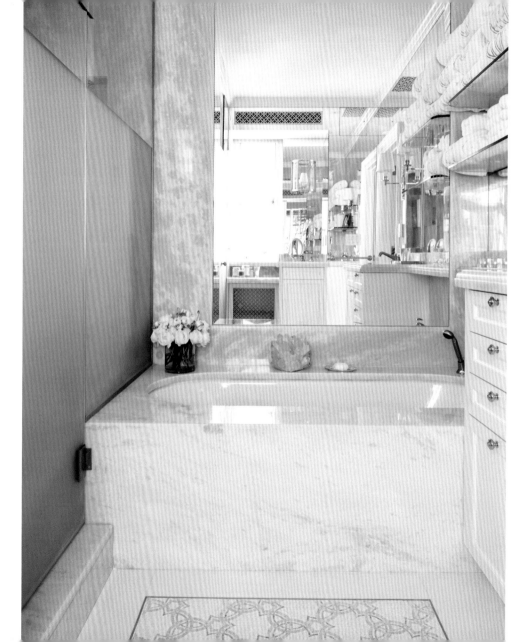

50

Does it get more posh and sophisticated than this? Onyx, an exotic translucent material, covers the floor and travels up the soaring walls as trim. Mirrored doors make the room look even larger.

51

This tub is based on nineteeth century style and is deep and capacious enough for two bathers.

52

Painted black-and-white stripes channel the spirit of the legendary decorator Dorothy Draper in an all-black-and-white master bathroom. The color combination is timelessly chic. ►

53

The cushy chaise and the TV above the mirrored vanity make this a room to spend hours in. Blue glass tiles and the clear-glass wallcovering are as soothing as the sea. A crystal chandelier adds a note of opulence.

54

A wall of vivid blue glass tile invigorates a master bathroom. Black-and-white river stone embedded in concrete adds graphic punch; it's often found in Moorish interior courtyards.

55

The Moorish motif carries over in the pointed arches and latticed doors on cupboards and in the trim on the vanity. The simplest of mirrors reflects a traditional globe lantern.

56

The mesmerizing patterns of Moroccan tile evoke the atmosphere of a traditional hammam. The massage tub is rimmed with quartzite. Swinging doors made of lattice panels lead to the water closet. ◄◄

57

Moroccan tile also covers the floor like a carpet and runs under the large vanity. The vanity's legs and lattice panels lend it a lighter, airier look.

58

A border of tiles runs like a ribbon around the room, adding more exotic textural interest and uniting all the spaces.

59

A long, hot, sensuous soak never looked so inviting. A blockbuster view frames the siren slipper tub, a modern rendition of a claw-foot tub.

60

The wall tiles have a beautiful ogee shape and a quietly iridescent gold glaze. Even on gray days, the room glows. Open the wine, light the candles!

61

An arched relief makes the vanity feel more like a piece of furniture. It's painted white with a strié on it for softening. Open spaces keep it from feeling too massive. Lavender towels play well with the gold wall tile.◄

62

Walls, floors, and door casings sheathed in marble, along with the ogee arches, have an old-world aura that calls to mind a Turkish bath.

63

A bath finds its femininity in watery blue walls, a 1940s French makeup mirror with a peachy glow, and glazed Moroccan cement tiles with shifting color like mother-of-pearl.

64

Arches frame four distinct areas—tub, toilet, sink, and shower. The cerused-oak vanity has a beachy, driftwood quality, as if it's been out in the wind and sea spray.

65

The blue of the polished Venetian plaster walls picks up the blue in the floor tiles. The Moroccan tiles are carried over to the tub enclosure, eliciting harmony and more iridescence in the room.

66

Like the tub surround, the vanity countertop is polished cast concrete in a neutral finish that goes well with the putty tone in the tiles. The unlacquered brass finish of the sink and tub faucets takes on the patina—and therefore the character—of age.

67

In a house with his-and-hers bathrooms, hers has a quietly elegant air, with a patterned rug, pedestal table, and vintage chest.

68

His is lined with bands of limestone and marble that continue around the room. Materials are luxurious without being glitzy and the bold stripes are masculine without being heavy.

69

A vintage rosewood console was fitted with a sink and topped with limestone. The medicine cabinet isn't obvious because the mirror is framed in rosewood to match the console.

70

There's nothing more indulging than a walk-in shower, and this one is practically a room within a room.

71

A master bath with masculine and feminine vanities brings back the well-groomed opulence of the 1930s. To create his vanity, a handsome Louis-Philippe burled-walnut commode was fitted with a small sink.

72

Stainless steel tiles mimic panels and mosaic moldings. An antique chair is given a modern twist with cotton cashmere.

75

Her vanity was put together from standard cabinetry. It was built to the same height as his commode, 39½ inches—higher than the norm, but you don't have to lean so far down.

76

Feet were added to the vanity to make it look like furniture, and a silvery finish was applied for an age-of-elegance feeling.

73

The floor extends into the shower, slanting gently toward the drain, so it doesn't need a curb to block the water. ▶

74

On open shelves, everything is handy—and you can create lovely vignettes with storage baskets, art or family photos, and flowers. ▶

77

The marble that is on her vanity was also used on the tub surround. The color of the window trim was matched to its creamy tone, which warms all the metal. Roman shades are automated: They go up at 9 a.m. and down at 9 p.m.

78

Drummond's Spey tub and standpipe take center stage, but the custom glass-and-steel shower stall, fabricated by Elite Remodeling, is equally eye-catching.

79

Inspired by a boutique, the closet's open shelves run from floor to ceiling along one wall. Doors were added in the center to create some closed storage.

80

The room was designed around strong elements and basic colors—just black, chocolate brown, and cream. The antique chaise is covered in Belgian linen.

81

Subway tile is used on the walls and behind the shelves, which gives a wonderful glow at night and you can see exactly what you're looking for.

82

Dark and light, masculine and feminine are in dramatic contrast in a master suite bath. The sleek white tub—a modern take on an old-fashioned Victorian slipper tub—plays off handsome, clubby walnut paneling, and the beaded chandelier injects a glimmery, girly element.

83

The room is doorless, but white-painted paneling conceals everything from view except the tub and bold graphic print.

84

An opaque glass wall lets light through to the toilet area while still ensuring privacy. A folding door is disguised as paneling to make it consistent with the walls. The floor is ceramic tile that looks like marble. ▶

85

Double showerheads were installed for a simultaneous husband-and-wife shower. The pipes give it the refreshing look of an outdoor shower.

86

The floor is in smaller tile squares. When doing a shower without a threshold, the floor has to be sloped for the water to drain, and smaller tile works better—the extra grout also helps make it more slip-resistant. The wall tiles have a metallic sheen.

87

The walnut vanity, designed to look like a bureau, is framed in Corian countertop. Sink faucets are beautiful and minimal. The high-gloss ceiling glows like poured milk.

88

An attic room is ingeniously transformed into a gentleman's bath and dressing room. To avoid closing in the space even more, the two areas are divided by a tiled half-wall with wall-mounted sinks. ◄◄

89

The shower curtain is suspended on a shower pan enclosure; it can be pulled around the basin or pushed aside with tiebacks.

90

A thirteen-foot-long antique counter with twenty-four drawers—dream storage—is the dressing area's centerpiece. Mirrors are glued to the backs of medicine cabinets, so they're mirrored on both sides.

92

Medicine chest mirrors slide upward, revealing shelving. Niches were carved into the walls for toiletries and towels. ◄

93

Over the sinks, faucets and handles are purposely mismatched. The red handles add industrial flair and a zingy accent.

91

The womblike tub has a clean simplicity and adds graceful curves to a bathroom dominated by angles. Wainscoting and eaves were tiled with dark gray grout for a more graphic effect.

94

Brown-and-white slab marble creates
an opulent, masculine mood in a man's
bathroom, much like a gentleman's club.

95

Bleached cherry walls,
rose aurora marble, and
lofty architecture give a
luxuriant air to a master
bathroom. Natural
light passes through the
frosted-glass mirror
surround, and the whole
mirror panel slides into
the wall.

96

Metallic paint cocoons the whole room—walls, trim, ceiling, even the exterior of the tub—in a silvery glow.

97

An aluminum wine table radiates sunlight falling on its surface. Indonesian pebbles composed of sandstone and onyx texturize the floor.

98

The chrome hardware, mirror frame, lantern, and accessories keep the tonal shimmer consistent. Baskets store towels under the double console washstands fitted with undermount sinks.

99

A whirlpool tub between his-and-hers vanities adds to the air of quiet luxury in the master suite of a lake house.

100

Walls are rough-cut plank pine, a wood with fabulous texture that changes shades or tones according to the way the light hits it.

101

Soft tones and subtle textures create an air of repose. Limestone floors, marble countertops, and alabaster urns reference ancient Roman materials.

102

The rays of an antique starburst mirror hung in a round window are echoed in a contemporary wheelback armchair.

103

The pale-honey hue of the plaster walls and ceiling and the limestone on the floor and tub surround exude a mellow glow that envelops you, as does the pleasing rhythm and weight of the arched niche. This is the essence of a soothing retreat.

104

Tropical luxury is the hallmark of a bathroom with a bank of windows over the tub. The niche and Ohio wood columns are an extra touch of grandeur. The deck stone surrounding the tub supplies more handsome texture.

105

Under a flowing arch, a freestanding tub takes center stage on the Calacatta marble floor. The delicate chandelier, creamy drapes, antique Turkish rug, and tree in a metallic pot are luxuriant elements that make the room transcend the utilitarian.

106

The beautiful lines of this freestanding oval tub are showcased in front of windows overlooking a garden. Its graceful silhouette is enhanced by the burnished cast-iron exterior. Tiger-print towels are folded over the rungs of bamboo ladders.

107

With a luscious cut-velvet screen backing the tub, the look is more dressing room than bathroom. Glamorous though it is, it was a pragmatic gesture, for privacy. If the window had been draped, the room would have been too dark.

108

A very small bath in a small one-room apartment was poshly dressed up by tenting it in fabric, taking it from claustrophobic to embracing.

Chapter 2 Spa-like

80

81

82

84

85

87

88

89

91

92

92

93

96

97

99

"THERE'S NOTHING LIKE A BATH THAT'S A DESTINATION, A ROOM WHERE YOU REALLY WANT TO SPEND TIME. YOU GO IN, LIGHT CANDLES, HAVE A LONG SOAK, AND TURN OFF YOUR BRAIN. WHAT CAN BE BETTER THAN THAT? NOTHING, FRANKLY."—BRIAN MCCARTHY

109

It's easy to imagine spending a whole day in a room that gives new meaning to the home spa. There's a soaking tub, a large steam shower, and enough room to set up a massage table. The grandly scaled space is part of a master suite.

110

Two chairs, a table, and a fireplace: the perfect spot for morning coffee while your hair dries.

111

The armoire holds toiletries and is a nice decorative element in the room.

112

The Art Deco–inspired side chairs are upholstered in terrycloth.

114

A spa room's plasterwork, limestone, and low lighting transport you to a different world, a different time, as though you're in a centuries-old public bathhouse in Italy. It's insular and dreamy—the fantasy of the good life.

113

In the bathroom and dressing area, rich deep apricot walls have tactile softness that makes you feel you're in the south of France. An Italian Rococo desk was transformed into an exquisite vanity table. ▶

115

In a glimmering master bath, silver-leaf tea paper on the ceiling reflects the glow of the chandelier, and mirrored chests converted into vanities reflect the luminous white marble and honey onyx floor.

116

Walls are Venetian plaster, which gives the room a spa feeling. Chairs are incredibly comfy, upholstered in a velvety terrycloth. It's a dreamy retreat.

117

Hard to believe this is a private bath—it's more like a spa retreat. A large, slanted window renders an open, airy greenhouse atmosphere.

118

The Italian porcelain soaking tub takes center stage and provides an unparalleled bathing experience. The movement of the marble floor tile veining is like an incoming tide.

119

Reflected in the vanity mirror is refined teak, soft and warm against all the cool stone. The wood, which absorbs moisture well, is also on the floor of the shower.

122

The countertop is a solid slab of glass, made from recycled bottles, imbued with metallic threads that sparkle.

120

Teak flooring is flush with walls of Thassos marble tile. You don't have to step over or down to get in the shower—you just step in. The ceiling is painted a pale, watery, spa-like blue.

121

A spectacular, large-scale, powder-coated chandelier meets the proportion of the tub and the showmanship of the floor.

123

It's the ultimate spa experience in a space designed expressly for a woman in an apartment with hers-and-his bathrooms. It's all about fantasy—spacious, sybaritic, serene.

124

Water fills the Japanese soaking/whirlpool tub from a splash-free ceiling-mount bath filler. There's also a walk-in shower with body sprays, steam, and music.

125

A zebrawood-and-marble vanity is topped with a rectangular porcelain sink. The mirror runs the length of the room. ◄

126

The tub's round shape is ultra-feminine. The windows have a lake view, and floating the tub against back-painted blue glass creates the feeling of floating out over the lake.

127

The zebrawood vanity in the "his" bath is a duplicate of hers, with the exception of the square vessel sink. Waxy Venetian plaster walls not only lend a mellow, fresco-finish look, they repel water.

128

A sink-to-ceiling strip of mirror between the windows is big enough for shaving without intruding on the city view. Chrome-and-glass pendant lights are so slender, they almost go away.

129

One-foot-square marble tiles line a shower equipped with a showerhead on the wall and a rain shower on the ceilings.

130

A ribbon of blue glass tiles wraps the bathroom and ripples like water. The watery frieze unifies the separate areas. The tub floats on wood blocks like a piece of sculpture.

133

A floor-mounted faucet doesn't encroach on the tub's pure lines.

131

The vanity is topped with a slab of honed marble with a six-inch apron front. That gives it more heft, which suits the scale of the room.

132

A pretty, feminine mirror adds a few curves. A ceramic garden stool by the tub could hold a drink and a candle.

134

Accessories, like this wooden tub tray, follow through on the simple, elemental aesthetic.

135

Tiles are laid in a running bond, adding a little movement.

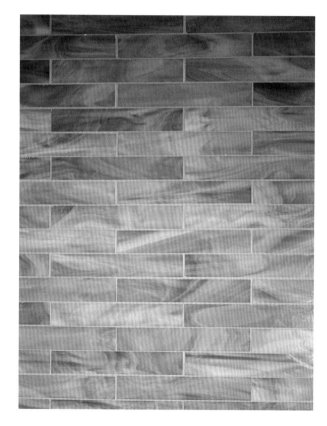

136

An open shelf in the vanity was sized for towels.

137

The mirror seems to float as well, with only a beveled edge instead of a frame. The shells on the sconces add another texture and become translucent in the light.

138

The sink faucet is the same sleek, curved style as the bathtub's.

139

Hooks hold towels trimmed with cotton binding, in the manner of fine men's shirts.

140

An arched niche houses a dual
soaking tub with aromatherapy,
chromatherapy, and hydromassage
features.

141

The expansive window makes the
bosky exterior part of the interior
and frames it like a painting.

143

The shower's mother-of-pearl banding is a repeat of the tile banding above the vanities. It was inspired by the mother-of-pearl detail on the vessel sinks.

142

Understated honey-vanilla limestone creates a calming, spa-like feeling. His-and-hers vessel sinks were placed on the clean, minimal vanities. A mirrored door reflects the lush green view.

145

Wallpapered like a bamboo garden, a master bath is like an escape to an exotic locale. The whirlpool tub accentuates the feeling of being removed from all your daily cares and woes.

144

Calacatta Tia marble wrapping the deep oval tub lends a spa-like feeling to the room. The framed fan coral adds color.

146

The lustrous finish of polished tile contrasts with the richness of dark wood for a bathroom that's transporting. An oval tub is lavished with handcrafted wood and marble.

147

A huge steam shower is like having your very own wellness center. The cool, clean lines of the solid chrome-plated brass have a sophisticated modernity that's set off by the classic basket-weave pattern of the floor tile. ▶

148

If a deep inhale and a long exhale were a bathroom, it would be this one: The soft luminosity of the colors and materials infuses it with serenity.

Chapter 3 Traditional & Transitional

103

105

107

109

112

115

116

117

118

119

120

121

127

128

131

"THE FINISHES IN TRADITIONAL BATHROOMS—CREAMY SUBWAY TILE, WHITE MARBLE, PAINTED WAINSCOTING— ARE COMFORTING IN THEIR FAMILIARITY AND 'RIGHTNESS,' AND THE SOFT CONTOURS OF THE FIXTURES ADD A SENSE OF EASE."—TOM SCHEERER

149

A husband and wife have their own bathrooms, but instead of doing two small showers, there's one big shower that separates them. Nickel fixtures and crystal knobs give her side a soft gleam.

150

His side is smaller and his floor tile is different, which individualizes the spaces. The faucet also has ebony handles, for a little heft, and the cabinet has twisted pulls.

151

The tub is on her side. Its style feels timeless, not too antique and not too contemporary, and the curve of the lip works well with the curve of the arch—a detail that softens the space and makes it more feminine.

152

The Calacatta marble tile has a border, like a rug, to make this area feel like a room within a room.

153

A show-stopping Louis-Philippe mirror is framed by traditional raised-panel cabinetry that adds elegant detailing to a master bath. Glass knobs add sparkle and a period touch.

154

The one bathroom in an apartment has to also function as the powder room, so it was designed to be slightly dramatic, and as elegant as possible.

155

A sconce and a lamp on the counter supply two different elements of light—one for primping, one for ambience.

156

Wainscoting and cabinets were painted a warm mahogany and the upper wall was painted a soft gold—a combo that adds both depth and a burnished glow to the room. ▶

157

Books cozy up any room. A mini faux library papers the wall of a snug bathroom and substantial dark blue fabric gives the impression of drapery more than it does a shower curtain. An antique rug substitutes for a bath mat.

158

A vintage dresser was painted black and given ring pulls for a campaign chest look. It's fitted with shallow drop-in sinks, so even the top drawers are useable.

159

A white tub against dark limestone walls sets up a crisp contrast in a master bathroom. The deep-seated slipper chair injects whimsy, and also holds extra towels.

160

A stool is a little luxury: It can be an end table for the tub—for candles, flowers, and a book.

161

Glossy dark-stained floors offer an anchoring contrast to the creamy walls and ceiling. They also pick up light from the French doors in the adjoining bedroom, and the window above the capacious soaking tub. The sink-stand was based on a French iron console.

162

The elaborate veining of marble supplies free-form pattern to the room. Curtains in a textured fabric frame the tub and when pulled create a private oasis.

163

An Hermes stool on an antique rug injects a soupçon of casual elegance to a traditional bath.

164

Country chic defines a guest bathroom, which has both an elemental simplicity and a polished prettiness. Chicken wire on the cabinet doors makes the snug room feel more open.

165

In a teenage boy's bath, wallpaper has the look of tile without the expense. To balance the small scale of the pattern, 12-by-12-inch floor tiles were laid on the diagonal to expand the space.

166

The front of the vanity is stained brown and the inside is painted black, creating symmetry with the browns and blacks in the granite on the floor and countertop.

167

Soft, curvy real tile was used in his younger sister's bath. The twirling pattern has movement reminiscent of pinwheels.

168

Full-length mirrors on both sides of the vanity reflect the one tiled wall, giving the illusion that all the walls are tiled. With such a fantastic focal point, the rest of the bath was given a white-cloud look.

169

Buoyant green wallpaper has a charming, youthful feeling and animates a bathroom that is shared by two preschool girls in a suburban house.

170

Another bathroom shared by two young girls got a happy jolt with energy when it was wallpapered with jaunty magenta vines.

171

Only a sink and shower inhabit a tiny bathroom, but the atmosphere couldn't be more feel-good. A zippy dotted wallpaper highlights the scalloped mirror, reflecting a girly pink shower curtain.

172

Pattern-on-pattern spiffs up a guest bath. In black and white, it has graphic appeal. Both the inlaid bone mirror and wallpaper have floral motifs that blend seamlessly.

173

Before blue-and-white fabric went up, the wall was a washed-out yellow—too bland for the intensity of the floor tile. A dumpy little horizontal mirror was replaced with one the same color and width of the sink. ▲

174

Concerned about humidity from hot showers and baths, a designer had his painter copy a wallpaper with a flowering quince motif on the bathroom walls. ◄

175

Wainscoting of decorative Portuguese glazed tiles steals the show in a master bathroom. The side chair is slipcovered in a complementary blue-and-white linen stripe. The room offers a fresh spin on a classic color combination.

176

Modern and country meet in a master bath built in a silo. The undulating curves of the vanity echo the shape of the planked walls and inject a sensuous balance to the stainless steel base.

177

Hurricane lantern sconces make for romantic candlelight soaks in the angular steel tub, which is big enough to accommodate two.

178

The big round mirror echoes the roundness of the sinks.

179

The claw-foot roll-top tub adds a period touch, but the big, open shower is the essence of contemporary.

180

Ojai river rock makes a powerful statement on the floor of a 1920 farmhouse bathroom. It's earthy but also edgy, especially juxtaposed with a shower door in the style of a casement window and a beaded chandelier.

181

The Navajo rug provides a vibrant burst of color as well as an authentic piece of indigenous Americana.

182

Dark and light are juxtaposed to
brilliant effect in a bath with a
seamless blend of traditional and
modern elements.

183

Repeating the floor's Calacatta
marble on the tub ledge provides a
linking visual harmony, and the long,
horizontal clerestory window repeats
the shape of the vanity. A leather
ottoman makes a soft landing for
towels or a temporary sit-down.

184

A cozy new master bathroom in a 1950s ranch house looks as if it has always been there—give or take a modern luxury or two. The basket-weave tile, wood wainscoting, and 1950s paintings all evoke the era.

185

The vanity, inspired by a mid-century modern credenza, is topped with Carrara marble and dressed up with brass pulls.

186

The mirror and sconce have a fine-boned elegance that lends an air of femininity and enhances the credenza feeling.

187

The bathtub has a simplicity and compactness that works well with the floor pattern and in a small space. The texture, made of volcanic limestone and resin, is extra smooth, like porcelain, but it isn't as costly and heavy.

188

The shower's pebble floor is relaxing, even therapeutic. A teak wood stool was added for holding towels.

189

In a traditional 1850 Cape Cod cottage, the guest bath feels authentic to the mid–nineteenth century, but also clean and modern.

190

Old-world style updated with twenty-first-century technology combines the best of the past and present in a bathroom that appeals to all the senses.

191

Subway tile is used on the walls and shower fixtures, from the Astaire collection by Newport Brass, and are arranged in a line. "It looks neat and clean that way," says designer Deirdre Doherty.

192

In a house with traditional bones, a wood-framed gothic arch backed by a brick wall makes a big impact in the master bath.

193

Dark wood trim adds a layer of warmth and gives the arched niche definition and charm. The contemporary freestanding faucet adds a sleek sculptural note.

194

Is it traditional, exotic, spa-like, natural? All of the above. When it comes to big gestures, not much tops this red-and-white chinoiserie wallpaper—it's happy but not at all overwhelming.

195

The rectangular acrylic tub is enveloped in solid teak that has handy built-in cubicles for bath linens.

198

This little black lacquered box of a bathroom is a surprising—and very sexy—treat for guests. A Regency ebony-and-bone mirror is propped against a mirrored wall that reflects the mirrored wall opposite, creating a seemingly infinite sequence of rooms.

199

Baskets, a scorched bamboo table, and bamboo shades add natural tones and textures and create a link with the outdoors.

196

Daylight filters through the translucent shelf unit, bouncing light off the mirrors and the gleaming countertop on the sleek vanity.

197

The shelves hold stacks of books—an original touch, and very useful when you want to settle in with a good novel for a nice, relaxing soak.

200

A master bath's mocha-brown walls play up the brilliant whites of a recycled tub, sheer curtains, and floor and shower tiles. The crystal light fixture is a 1980s update of old-school glamour.

201

White, black, and gray have the power of a contemporary fine-art photograph. Floral motifs are an eye-catching twist on classic black-and-white tile floors.

202

The antique crystal chandelier in the shape of a ship contributes a period feeling and a snappy bit of wit—and it draws the eye upward to the skylight.

Chapter 4 Modern

135

137

138

141

142

143

144

145

146

148

149

151

154

157

159

"TODAY'S MODERN BATHROOM ISN'T A STARK ENVIRONMENT. LIGHT, A SENSE OF OPENNESS, AND FIXTURES THAT BECOME SCULPTURE MAKE IT FEEL SYBARITIC— YOUR OWN PRIVATE SPACE MEANT FOR LUXURIATING."—VICENTE WOLF

203

Striated marble marches dramatically across the floor, over the tub, and up the wall. To balance the high impact, everything else is elegantly understated.

204

The shower curtain hangs from a recessed track in the ceiling to eliminate the visual intrusion of a rod.

205

Walnut doors frame a wide-trough sink fitted into a wall-mounted, lacquered vanity. The frameless medicine cabinet, recessed into the wall, has interior lighting and a sliding door that lifts up. Single-lever faucets in polished chrome complete the streamlined look.

206

A minimalist waterfall tub filler with no backplate appears to come straight out of the wall, giving the niche above the tub a fountain effect.

207

A sophisticated play of light and dark adds luminosity and drama to a small guest bath, clad in two types of mosaic tiles. The clean, crisp lines of the cube tub are echoed in the sink, set into a vanity topped with Indian Ivory limestone, which is also on the floor.

208

Lighting was incorporated underneath the floating vanity, adding to the glow. It also works as a nightlight.

210

The creamy, white undulating marble tile continues down to the shower floor, where it becomes mini squares—good traction for bare feet.

209

Polished chrome faucets and valves, inspired by traditional early-twentieth-century fixtures, have a gleaming simplicity.

211

A liner of white bronze separates the two tiles and has a wavy surface itself, which makes it feel handmade.

212

Walls and surfaces are made of crystallized glass tiles, but in this luminous room, the drama is really on the chevron-patterned marble floor.

213

Brown and white zigzags were chosen instead of the more usual black and white because the color combo felt less rigid. It's a directional pattern, pointing to the window.

214

The medicine cabinets are behind the mirror over the vanity. On each side, a panel of mirror slides back to reveal the shelves.

216

Another mirror was added above the toilet to open up the space. There is a transparent layering going on with the mirrors, the window, and the glass shower door that makes the space feel three-dimensional. ▶

215

A cubic seat in the shower looks clean and pure. Bath products are always within easy reach in a convenient niche just above it.

217

Veins of gold ripple against the dramatic black background of Nero Portoro marble. It's an operatic stone, and makes for a bathroom that's pure theater. ▶

218

A small master bathroom has the shadowy darks and lights of a Vermeer painting, creating mood. The sculpted horse's head silhouetted against the window adds more artistry. The trough-like sink has a powerful presence in the compact space.

219

Dark brown marble in the bath enclosure, walnut on the vanity, and polished terrazzo tiles give a man's bath an aura of refined masculinity. The room has a grand quality because of the very tall ceiling.

220

Trim around the top of the marble brings the eye down a bit. The wood is protected by a marine-grade varnish.

221

The subtle veining of the marble doesn't overwhelm its rich background color. ◀

222

Sink fixtures are sleek and simple. The walnut gives the vanity visual interest and weight, and warms up the room.

223

Two hospital tracks are recessed into the ceiling for two shower curtains. The one on the interior side functions as a window curtain.

224

A huge mirrored cabinet provides an unusual architectural element to a stylishly tailored bath. As it reflects parallel lines of recessed lighting, there's a semblance of a room beyond the room.

225

A basin alcove radiates a golden glow from the glazed walls in an elegantly appointed bath. A lamp several feet high lights the area like a sconce. It's mounted on the stone counter, and the faucet is mounted on the mirror above the glass basin.

226

Glass doors with an almost-not-there frame divide the shower from the rest of the bathroom without diminishing the sense of space. The simplicity of the form is repeated in the mirror.

227

There's no threshold, so the stone-tiled floor flows uninterrupted. Slender towel bars on the vanity doors are stylishly handy.

228

Tiles in a master bath are reminiscent of a fluted column and add texture to the natural palette.

229

The purist above-counter marble sink, above-floor vanity, and one-piece streamline toilet are in keeping with the modernist vibe.

230

The no-frills sink and medicine cabinet enhance the linear simplicity of the space.

231

Caesarstone, a durable quartz surface, clads the tub, countertop, and window frame of a children's bathroom in a contemporary farmhouse, creating an orderly geometry and earthy texture against the lighter neutral tones.

232

The room doubles as a guest bath, so it had to be both kid-friendly and sophisticated. Extra-tall medicine cabinets echoing the shape and scale of the window keep clutter at bay. It's an exercise in simplicity and restraint.

233

A big Formica vanity was removed from a very small bathroom and replaced with a modern console sink. A mirror hangs in front of the window. The wall is covered with linen, giving the space a handsome tailored appearance.

234

A bathroom for two features matching bowl basins and a wall-to-wall console. The limited wall space on each side of the windows was solved with tall, narrow mirrors.

237

Warm wood and clean-lined simplicity give a bathroom in a mid-century house a 1950s Scandinavian feel. A wall-mounted faucet and modular sink complete the look.

235

Shipshape and streamlined, this thoroughly modern bathroom is evocative of a yacht.

236

Terrazzo tile plays off the white vessel sinks and vanity, and dark wood trim creates simple geometric patterns on the painted walls.

238

The strict, rectilinear lines, poured-concrete tub, and swimming pool tiles convey a sturdy masculinity. A carved-out niche for bath products helps keep the aesthetic spare.

239

A bathroom in a glass-tower apartment is a celebration of modernism executed with elegance. The squares of mirrors climbing the high walls complement the shape of the frosted panels in the doors.

240

The curve of the cast-concrete tub balances all the hard angles, bringing a balancing softness to the room.

241

Placing a cast-concrete tub on a concrete slab inside the glassed shower enclosure makes it a stunning focal point. With the honed limestone floors and walls, the sheer shades, and the openness, it's a calm, ethereal space.

242

Shower walls are lined with reverse-painted glass tile, which gives a sense of depth and luminosity to the color—a deeply aquatic effect. The stool brings a spa element to the space.

243

Steel-and-glass enclosures for two showers (the second one is reflected in the mirror) are made of classic casement windows. We're used to seeing them on flat elevations, so the three-dimensional design creates a delightful visual kick.

244

The many shades of gray in marble subway tile form an improvisational pattern in an open shower. A partial wall allows for partial privacy.

245

Stripes are a nice graphic design element than can bring movement and pattern to a room, but not in a busy way. The glossy tile, which reflects light, and the clear glass shower enclosure give the small room an open, airy mood.

246

The showerhead slides up and down, accommodating guests of various heights. A two-prong swing-arm towel rack takes up a fraction of the wall space of a standard towel bar.

248

Besides the big, bold stripes, a trough-style washbasin is another overscale gesture that adds oomph to the tiny space. It's wall-mounted, so it doesn't interfere with the flow of the stripes.

247

A square handle is one of many clean, rectilinear elements that contribute to the clean-lined, modern feeling. ▶

249

Penny round tiles on the floor give you a lot of little pops of shine, and a good gripping quality as well. The round shape softens and balances all the rectilinear shapes.

Chapter 5 Pure & Simple

163

165

166

167

168

170

171

172

173

175

176

179

180

183

185

"A BATHROOM HAS GOT TO BE PEACEFUL. IT'S THE ONE ROOM IN YOUR HOUSE WHERE YOU CAN LOCK THE DOOR AND RETREAT. ABOVE ALL, THERE HAS TO BE AN EFFICIENCY. AND IT HAS TO BE REALLY CLEAN!"—BARBARA SALLICK

250

By marrying a charming vintage feeling with modern all-white airiness, an updated bathroom in a 1920s Cape Cod cottage is as pure and refreshing as a bar of Ivory soap.

251

The view from the spa tub has a no-nonsense look, but with the deck on it, there's a sense of stepping into another—very therapeutic—room.

252

Frameless mirrors float over oval sinks fitted into pristine, high-polish marble tops. Traditional hardware is in hand-brushed nickel, which doesn't show watermarks or fingerprints.

253

Walls of horizontal shiplap, a paneling often used in houses in the 1920s, have an unpretentious warmth.

254

The paneling is painted high-gloss white, making it easy to clean. The finish also stands up well to water and contrasts wonderfully with the brushed nickel.

255

Behind its neat façade, a storage cabinet with opaque glass panels conceals a welter of toiletries.

256

Tall vertical mirrors mimic the high windows and accentuate the majestic height of the all-white room. White reflects light, making the space feel illuminated from within.

257

The tub has a pure, organic beauty. The art piece hanging above it is a whimsical papier-mâché sculpture—an homage to a stylish, shoe-loving woman.

258

A master bath is a soothing retreat, with sumptuous but minimal furnishings. Tiles in a chevron pattern set off the strong, sculptural shape of the tub.

259

What a serene, pretty oasis. The glossy pale pink walls pick up on the pale pink accents in the marble tile. The narrow, flat edges of the sleek cube tub allow for a spacious interior.

260

Opulent and luminous play off cool and airy. All the surfaces shimmer. Walls are white milk glass; the floor is glass mosaic.

261

Even the fabric used for the blinds has a thin gold Lurex thread running through it, and the tub fittings have a finish that's between gold and silver.

262

Mirrors above mirrors double the light coming into a long, narrow bathroom. Creamy colors give it a soothing richness.

263

This master bathroom is the very definition of purity and simplicity. The claw-foot tub is original to the late-1800s house. The shade filters light without blocking it.

264

White-painted wainscoting, a white floor, pedestal sinks, and a claw-foot tub give a master bath a fresh but timeless appeal.

265

Pure and simple as a Shaker church, the bathroom of a seaside house gets its airy look from high ceilings and walls painted pale blue.

266

The mosaic tile floor was designed on a computer with CAD software and manufactured in one piece, like a carpet.

267

A guest bathroom is a pampering bounty for out-of-towners, with its enameled cast-iron built-in tub and rain showerhead.

268

Practicality meets charm in a small bathroom, where everything is built-in, precise, and in apple-pie order.

269

The beadboard-clad walls and ceiling, painted in a satin finish, provide a stylishly inviting cottage-in-the-country look.

270

You can be at the beach no matter where you are. Beadboard and a white painted floor—helped along by a basket of white coral—give a master bath the attitude of an old seaside house. Amazing what a coat of white paint can do.

271

A barn-style mountain house provides a soaring space flooded with light from clerestory windows and an eye-level round window.

272

Built-in shelves hold family photos and towels—keeping them handy after a nice, long respite in the soaking tub.

273

A period-style pedestal tub with modern functionality is the main show in a plainspoken farmhouse bathroom. Rustic and refined marry very well.

274

To update a 1940s bathroom, the beige tub was glazed white, Carrara marble tiles were added, and a two-leg double-console sink was installed.

275

A floor of Carrara marble slabs and waterproof plaster on all the walls create a monolithic feel: The effect is Zen and peaceful.

276

The limed-oak vanity is wall-mounted, extending the expanse of the floor and adding to the airiness of the room.

277

Double sinks have ample room between them in a long, wall-to-wall, clean-lined vanity. Multiple sconces punctuate mirrors and art.

278

Round baskets holding bath linens soften the lines and repeat the shape and tone of the lampshades.

279

Instead of a bulky built-in, the vanity is basically a simple freestanding table with teak slats on the bottom. With all the storage, there was no need for a medicine cabinet. ▶

280

It looks as if you could float across the Atlantic in the soaking tub, like children in a fairy tale. Setting it on an angle lightens the room and takes advantage of the view.

282

Giving a beachy feeling, a border of interlocking pebbles rims the room, along with a baseboard of ceramic tiles with coral pebble detail. The same white mosaic is on the shower floor.

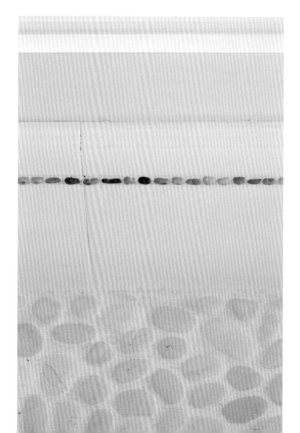

281

Glass walls make it feel as if the shower takes up less space. The glass is sealed with silicone to keep it watertight, and there's a clear plastic gasket on the door. But if water did happen to escape, it would not hurt the marble on the floor.

283

What's more pampering than a toasty, fluffy towel? It's easy to do with a warming drawer like this one.

284

A master bath is modest in size and modest in decoration, but it's also classic and timeless. A half-wall gives the toilet area privacy but also airiness, and adds architecture to the space.

285

An exposed thermostatic system makes showering as much of a luxurious pleasure as a soak in the tub. It's warmed by the richness and creaminess of the handmade glazed tile. Art in an elaborate frame lends a touch of the unexpected to the room.

286

A tiny, ho-hum alcove was transformed into a dazzler with a lustrous 1928 cast-iron pedestal sink from a salvage yard, and a 1920s French trifold mirror. ▶

287

The pair of vanities opposite the shower and topped with 1¼-inch-thick white marble are suggestive of consoles in an entry hall.

289

A bathroom squeezes maximum luxury out of a small space. It's blitzed floor to ceiling with 4-by-12-inch marble bricks laid with straight rather than staggered joints. Amazing the feeling of indulgence you get with massive quantities of the same material.

288

A master bath in a romantic wine-country house is simplicity itself, and a lesson in the transformative power of a single flower in a vase.

290

A city bathroom is kept clean and spare, but Calacatta marble wainscoting brings to it a hint of opulence.

291

The pedestal sink increases a sense of openness, and the pivot mirror allows for different viewing angles.

292

Pure, simple planes of marble and glass create a peaceful bathroom in an urban apartment. The honed marble that surrounds the tub becomes a seat inside the shower.

293

The mirrored backsplash goes all the way up to the ceiling, as do the pocket doors, to make the room feel taller.

294

Wall-mounted faucets were used so as not to interrupt the pure slab of marble. It also makes the countertop easier to clean. The toilet is mounted on the wall as well, for the same reasons.

Chapter 6 Nostalgic

189

190

191

192

193

194

195

196

197

198

200

202

204

206

209

"THERE'S JUST SOMETHING ABOUT THE PATINA OF AN OLD BRASS FAUCET OR THE WELL-WORN SURFACE OF AN ANTIQUE MARBLE VANITY THAT I FIND APPEALING— THAT SENSE OF AUTHENTIC HISTORY THEY BRING TO A BATH."—KEN FULK

295

A strong current of romance flows through a master bath designed with an authentic period look. The faux-bamboo mirror is from the 1870s, and the Arts-and-Crafts tiles and chandelier are from the 1920s. The fern fabric on the walls brings nature in.

296

The vanity is an assemblage of wonderfully compatible antiques—a painted 1770s desk, a Gustavian bench, and a bone-and-mother-of-pearl mirror.

297

A window meant there wasn't enough wall space for a mirror above a guest-bath sink in the same house, so a shaving-style mirror was mounted upside down on the ceiling.

298

Everything in this master bath evokes a centuries-old Tuscan house. The patina of the plaster walls and reclaimed blue shutters imbues the niche with character. ◄

299

An antique marble double sink adds age and architectural presence to a French country-style bathroom. Hooks instead of towel bars suit the room's historical feeling.

300

Floating in front of French doors, an enameled cast-iron pedestal tub combines style with soul.

301

An antique cast-iron French bathtub heightens the period feel of a bathroom in an 1881 farmhouse.

302

The bergère, marble-topped table, landscape painting, and bureau-style vanity turn it into a stay-awhile refuge. The arched window was installed to bring architectural interest.

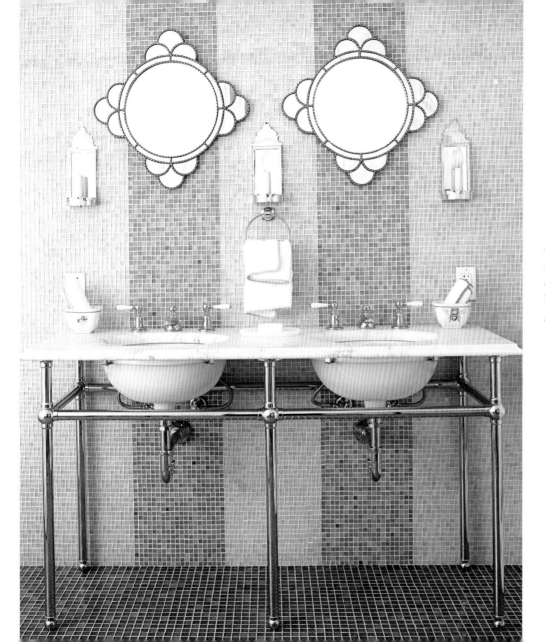

303

An abundance of glass mosaic tiles covers the floor and the wall behind a five-leg double washstand based on an early-1900s form. The amber stripes break up the large space. Deco mirrors are a fanciful flourish.

304

An antique chair covered in terrycloth melds function with chic. It's paired with another antique—a side table holding hand towels.

305

The footed oval cast-iron tub was hand-painted by a decorative artist. Cascading folds of bath sheets hanging from multiple hooks at two different heights create their own kind of art.

306

A Belle Epoque console sink, a 1940s French mirror, and Art Deco sconces impart a Parisian sensibility. The graceful curves of the scalloped mirror pick up on the curves of the sink's legs.

307

Capturing a romantic vision of the past, a bathroom in a historic cottage has an antique claw-foot tub set across from double French doors that open to a courtyard. The sink base is an eighteenth-century French buffet.

309

A master bath in a country house is trimmed in dark gray to create contrast and highlight classic architectural details.

310

A dainty Elsie de Wolfe–style chair and a pair of surreal photographs create their own kind of contrast.

308

Spatter wallpaper looks just right in an eighteenth-century beach cottage. It's reminiscent of the spatter-painted floors often seen in Colonial Cape Cod homes—they hide a multitude of sandy footprints. Think of it as a modern expression of early Americana. ►

312

A sink with drainboard, formerly in the kitchen, takes on new life as a vanity in an attic bathroom. The skirt fabric repeats the wallpaper pattern.

314

An antique sink with antique fixtures maintains the spirit and character of the house.

311

A pair of vintage medicine cabinets hangs about double antique sinks in the master bathroom of a large centuries-old country house. China matting has an inviting humility.

313

Pink walls and pink silk upholstery on a slipper chair bestow a rosy blush of femininity on a guest bathroom.

315

Instead of side-by-side sinks, two
sinks facing each other from opposite
sides of the room allow for paneling
under the window, which creates a
small shelf for bottles and toiletries
and contributes to the intended flavor
of an old beach bungalow.

316

The curtains are almost as fine as
a linen napkin, and hung on the
lightest rod. The painting of the nude
and the mahogany pot cupboard
inject wit and weight to the room.

317

Old-fashioned looks remarkably fresh in a 1930s lake house. The white-painted wooden medicine cabinet and chair and the green-painted wood floor conjure up images of summer camp. The two-leg washstand is new, but it's based on a style from the early 1900s.

318

Vintage charcoal portraits look as if they've always been at home on the wood planking in a classic old California rancher's cottage. So does the cross-handle faucet, even if it's contemporary.

319

An insect chart hangs above an iron tub from a salvage yard in a nineteenth-century farmhouse's master bathroom.

320

Planed-down boards from a nineteenth-century barn, an old-fashioned-style tub, a two-leg pedestal sink, and 1920s furniture bestow a classic-cottage feel to a large bathroom in a renovated 1980s beach house. The Flokati rug gives it a bedroom coziness.

321

A beach-house bathroom that's pure fun! Red accents are a bright, vivacious addition and a canvas sling chair plays along with the laid-back vibe. The old pedestal sink summons the nostalgia of a barber pole.

322

The master bathroom of a 1920s Florida house has a relaxed, friendly atmosphere suggestive of summer vacations in unpretentious beach cottages.

323

Wooden blinds pick up on the exposed wood ceiling, and faded teal walls set off the fresh whites of the claw-foot tub, mirror, and triple-chair settee.

324

Matte black paint revitalizes an old claw-foot tub in a Craftsman bungalow. Dark walls were brightened with light gray paint on the beadboard wainscoting and white paint above.

325

A trio of hooks instead of towel bars feels appropriate to the age and style of the room.

326

Imagine sinking down into neck-high water in this 1860s antique zinc-lined copper tub. A Chinese birdcage hung from the ceiling adds another element of delight.

327

Walls were coated with plaster and left unprimed and untreated. Then they were given a coat of lime wash mixed with natural pigments for Provençal charm.

328

In the "hers" bathroom of a nineteenth-century house, a freestanding oval bathtub—based on high-sloping nineteenth-century French copper tubs—has a gleaming presence in the gracefully simple room.

329

A nineteenth-century Italian chinoiserie-style painting over the footed soaking tub inspired the restful blue color palette. Why consign fine art to the living room? ▶

330

An armchair, a ceramic
stool, an aged Persian rug,
herringbone wallpaper,
and Roman shades create a
sitting room atmosphere in
a seaside cottage.

331

Living way out in the country,
you can bathe in the light, but silk
taffeta shades are there just in case.
The exterior of the bathtub—
modeled after a French boat
tub—is painted blue, a harmonious
complement to the antique rug.

332

Step into the burnished copper tub, and it feels as if you've stepped into another era. An antique Italian chair follows the curve. The inlaid Indian armoire, Chinese garden stool, and Turkish rug add global appeal.

333

The past steps into the present with elegant ease. A Victorian art glass pendant and side chair are in good company with a vintage-style tub. The shades are trimmed in a Greek-key design—a timeless motif—giving them a classic, finished look.

Chapter 7 Natural

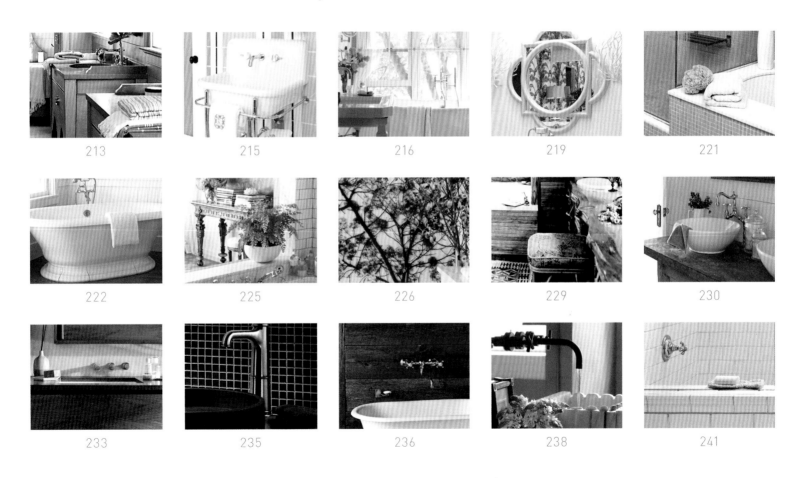

213

215

216

219

221

222

225

226

229

230

233

235

236

238

241

"NATURE APPEALS TO MY PLAYFULNESS.
I'VE USED SIMPLE PEBBLES TO CLIMB
THE FACE OF A BATHTUB, A BRANCH TO
HOLD TOWELS, OYSTER SHELLS AND RIVER
ROCKS TO LINE A SHOWER STALL.
AND DON'T GET ME STARTED ON
WATER PLAY!"—MIMI MCMAKIN

334

Bathed in leafy green, this old-fashioned room says "cabin in the woods." It feels like part of the scenery, as though you're outside amid the trees.

335

A simple, spare lantern hanging from a rope cord is a great combination of modern and rustic. The sconces, too, are on the edge of modern, but the shades take them back in time.

336

A breezy green paisley wallpaper has an out-of-doors quality without taking away from the beautiful marble tiles in the expansive shower enclosure.

339

Outdoor sconces make their way inside and flank a forged-iron mirror above the utilitarian washbasin. Frosted glass inset in the door lets more light in.

337

Such cheerfulness! A pool house bathroom is striped from floor to ceiling in green tile reflective of the surrounding landscape. It's an inventive, perky look.

338

To avoid breaking up the visual continuity of the room, the shower wall is frosted only in the middle.

340

Green porcelain tiles are a harmonious link to the abundant greenery framed like a painting by the window next to the shower. Their sheen is so reflective, it acts like a second window.

341

A wall of windows looking onto a lushly verdant wooded area creates the exhilarating feeling of being in your very own, very private tree house.

342

This bathroom takes its inspiration from forests, mountains, and streams. A fluted oak vanity, topped with white granite, is paired with clean, modern fixtures.

343

The undulating pattern of carved limestone tile has a rippling-water effect on the wall. Glass mosaic tiles on the shower floor are like stones at the bottom of a lake.

344

The ceiling is high, so wooden panels were added to frameless medicine cabinets to echo the proportions of the room.

345

Recesses for towels make the large wood vanity feel lighter. And there's something so casual about simply grabbing a towel off an open shelf.

346

You're always on island vacation with a bathroom painted in big, bold, green stripes, reminiscent of a classic beach cabana.

347

A predominance of white makes a bathroom feel really clean, and green adds life. The fern wallpaper creates an instant tropical rain forest, and coral sconces help evoke a holiday mood.

348

Shelves with white coral, grasscloth that looks like sand, and a rush chair create an island atmosphere—you can imagine yourself whisked away to the Bahamas. The chair, with its terrycloth cushion, makes a little spa corner for sitting after a bath.

349

Swathing a bathroom in blue imparts the feeling of being immersed in a clear blue sea. The glass mosaic tiles are installed to dramatic effect on the walls, floor, and tub surround of the spa bath.

350

The blue of these walls also suggests an ocean expanse. A round mirror that's like a giant porthole not only makes the bathroom feel much larger, it steals the show.

351

In a country-house guest bath, the cool blue tiles on the walls and ceiling of the shower enclosure evoke the bay waters of the Pacific Northwest. The floor and surround, window accent, and countertop are blue-gray Carrara marble.

354

Open the porthole window, and you feel as if you're outdoors.

352

A bunk-room bath in a beach house is fitted with lockers for family members and guests. Faucets on classic cast-iron sinks were stripped down to the brass.

353

The stripe on the towels echoes the wall paneling, painted in alternating flat and semigloss stripes.

355

Talk about a room with a view! Earth-toned tiles frame the dazzling waterscape but don't compete with it. Every soak in the tub rivals being in a first-class cabin on an ocean liner. ◄

356

A master bedroom in a seaside cottage looks out on the ocean, so the wall to the bathroom was opened for an unobstructed view of the water from the tub.

357

If you don't have a view, invent one!
A photograph of cherry blossoms on
glass creates a window where there is
none. Real blossoms on the tub ledge
amplify the illusion of a view. ▶

358

In a house inspired by the simple
country buildings of Belgium, the
bathroom has an earthy elegance. A
bubbles-up-to-your-chin bathtub with
three garden views is shaded by wood
blinds, whose shadows throw more
stripes onto the striped rug.

359

In a beach house with the character of a modern Scandinavian cabin, the tub is placed on a slight diagonal, with a view of the dunes. It's a moment of romance and surprise, like a candlelight dinner in a barn.

360

Midnight blue spruces up an antique claw-foot tub in the cedar-clad bathroom of a rural cottage.

361

The shower curtain can wrap around the tub, enveloping in an instant cocoon. A mirror lightens the expanse of brown wood.

362

Sunlight pouring into a cozy master bathroom in a mountain house intensifies the warmth of varnished pine beadboard swaddling almost every surface.

363

A playful mood overtakes the guest bath; walls were covered in brown kraft paper, then hand-painted with a snow flurry. Strips of birch bark cover vanity drawers and twigs branch out whimsically from the mirror.

364

In a late-nineteenth-century mountain house, a man's bathroom clad in old cypress strikes a cabin-like—and masculine—note. Framed art breaks up the expanse of brown and keeps it from feeling overpowering.

365

A weathered old console couldn't be more fitting for a humble farmhouse bathroom. There's a dynamic interplay between the worn zinc top and the crisp white vessel sinks.

366

A dark stone floor brings an element of the outside into a bathroom—a very European thing to do. It's complemented by the heavy black frame on the art.

367

The natural texture of baskets also brings a feeling of the outdoors in, as do raffia shades that filter the light.

368

Baskets are a great everyday item: They can be used for storage—towels, toiletries—or as a hamper or wastebasket.

369

A small but efficient master bath has a quiet, organic beauty. The long, lean horizontal lines of the wood cabinet keep it from looking weighty and blocky.

370

Teak on the floor and encasing the tub makes the space feel like a rustic Japanese farmhouse bathroom. ▶

371

A polished teak top and surround give sleek substance to a tub, elevating it to the status of furniture.

372

The sink and shower floor are also lined with teak, giving the room the serene atmosphere of a spa with natural warmth.

373

As an homage to the owner's love of horses, a SeaOtter Japanese ofuro soaking tub in redwood was made in the style of an old wooden trough. The wallpaper's imagery of blurry trees brings in another outdoorsy touch. A Missoni rug makes a colorful fashion statement.

374

Carved from volcanic slate and honed to a soft, smooth finish, this basin tempts you to run your fingers over it again and again. Paired with the Nakashima-like free-form wood base, its beauty is all the more evident.

375

In this country bathroom, it's all about the warm, reclaimed barn wood on the walls. Rustic never looked so chic.

376

A cupboard with barn doors hides a washer and dryer.

377

The stone-clad shower takes advantage of indoor-outdoor living: It's open to nature and the refreshing cleanliness of country air.

378

Against a mirrored wall, white matte marble and black lacquer are a beautiful pairing in a cottage bathroom.

379

Water falls from a black wall-mount faucet into the antique scalloped sink, placed on a leggy console that makes the small room feel larger.

380

Just outside the glass doors
of a master bathroom is
a (very) private shower.
Protected on one side
by a tall cast-concrete
screen and on the other
by a low wall of the same
unfinished cedar used in
the interior, the space
feels cool, yet sauna-like.
Mahogany flooring creates a
barefoot-smooth deck and a
comfortable bench as well.

382

Tucked under a staircase, a guest bath has slatted teak floors in the shower. The most minimal fixtures were used, including a body-spray showerhead recessed into the ceiling.

381

In the master bath, a wall-mounted toilet is concealed by a skirted sink. The shower opens to a private outdoor deck.

383

A nearly alfresco shower has French doors that open onto a walled garden. A side table with a hammered bronze finish introduces industrial chic to the breezy space.

384

A shower in a guesthouse invites couples in for an invigorating downpour with double rain showerheads. Clad in handmade field tile and filled with natural light, it has the summery aspect of an outdoor shower.

Chapter 8 Powder Rooms

245

246

249

250

253

255

256

259

261

263

264

265

267

268

271

"A FABULOUS POWDER ROOM
MAKES GUESTS FEEL SPECIAL.
IT'S A SPACE WHERE YOU
CAN EXPRESS YOURSELF,
BE CREATIVE, REALLY GO FOR IT!
I PERSONALLY LOVE USING WALLPAPER
BECAUSE IT ADDS SO MUCH
STYLE AND PERSONALITY."—MEG BRAFF

385

Powder rooms are places where you can go all out in an exuberant way—with pattern, color, drama, bling!

386

A high-impact geometric wallpaper in a bright ocean blue is the very definition of zest and zing.

387

Zigs and zags, diamond and dots: A wallpaper in variegated shapes and tones jazzes up the room, proving that strong pattern is a great way to bring life to a nondescript space.

388

The quatrefoil mirror and semicircular sink lend a simple curvaceous presence and counterpoint to the geometrics.

389

Black, white, and gold hexagonal wallpaper injects a big dose of pizzazz. Sconces of crystal tubes and brass lend a modernist handcrafted simplicity to the room.

391

Chinoiserie wallpaper and a brass shadow-ball light give this room a sparking exoticism. The sink echoes the shape of the light.

390

Red chinoiserie spices up a powder room. A standard-issue mirror would be all wrong on a wall with such spirit. It calls for one with an equally enticing personality.

392

Wrapped in ginger jar wallpaper, the room is a balance of the exotic and traditional. An actual porcelain vase reflected in the leather-framed mirror is a witty visual pun.

393

Marbleized paper and a 1940s French metal mirror complement the vintage marble sink and antique fixtures.

394

An extravagantly ornamented shield mirror was painted purple to match the orchids on the elegant wallpaper.

395

The peacock-feather wallcovering lends an exuberant energy to a powder room in an old-world Park Avenue apartment. The motif inspired the embroidery on the guest towel.

396

It might be pushing the envelope to paper a big room in such a graphic wallpaper, but in a powder room, it wows guests.

397

The compact hatbox toilet is a space saver—it integrates the tank and bowl.

398

A tiny space is given the royal treatment with antiques, chandeliers, and large-scale florals. Antiqued mirror panels on the sink wall and a silver-leafed Louis-Philippe mirror multiply the rows of dahlia blooms on the wallpaper. For a little surprise, the ceiling was lacquered turquoise.

399

The oversize motifs of floral wallpaper and a geometric mirror punch up the room. Liberal dashes of white keep everything light and airy.

400

This sweet cotton print is about as country French as you can get without using toile. It's fabric—backed with paper and pasted on—a slightly more dressed look than wallpaper.

401

The gilt frames on the mirror and photograph and the brass-and-leather two-tiered étagère give the room a furnished feeling.

402

Palm frond wallpaper feels fun and tropical, in a sophisticated way. The contrast of the crisp white vanity against colorful walls is cheerful, bright, and happy.

403

A small, weirdly shaped powder room under stairs was wrapped in wallpaper to make it feel bigger and more unified. Swimming with koi, the paper makes it feel as if you're in an underwater fairy tale.

404

Blending merriment with luxe, embroidered dragonflies swoop all over a silk wallcovering and in reflections of the glam mirrored vanity.

405

A decorative artist painted a mural on these walls, with a bird strategically perched on the faucet. An old washstand was fitted with a white porcelain sink.

406

Instead of ripping out dated and unappealing tilework, the space was rehabilitated with a pleated cotton stripe hung from a ceiling-mounted hospital track. The fabric also skirts the vanity.

407

A powder room takes on a quietly rich look, like fine jewelry, when walls are glazed in silver leaf. The polished brass vessel lavatory adds more jewel-like sparkle.

408

Pieces of antiqued mirror, embellished with rosettes and reflecting the soft glow from the shaded sconce, lend a smoky mystery to the space.

409

The room radiates a romantic and flattering glow from a wall of glass tiles in gold leaf. Guests are likely to linger in front of the mirror.

410

Marine life is a familiar powder-room theme, especially in oceanside houses. Beachcombing yielded this extraordinary vanity, a shell-encrusted fantasy. ▼

411

Mother-of-pearl tiles suffuse a powder room with an opalescent luster. The ornate mirrored vanity is fitted with an enormous clamshell for a sink. ◄

412

A harmony of shiny and matte, natural and industrial, old and new. A gleaming chrome spigot faucet punctuates the divide between the vessel sink and white coral mirror.

413

The mirror is behind an antique Italian window grille—not what you'd expect, but it's a winner, even if it's not ideal for refreshing your lipstick.

414

An old honed marble sink shows all the dings and splotches of age, which make it even more beautiful.

415

Imbued with the spirit of an old Tuscan villa, this tiny space speaks volumes about the beauty of patina.

416

An aura of soul, grace, and history permeate the room. Above an antique marble basin hangs a Baroque Italian mirror flanked by leafy candle sconces.

417

An iron garden urn was brought indoors and reinvented as a sink. A stone platform raises the urn's inset basin to conventional sink height.

418

A weathered urn with an aged patina and a classic pan fountain—installed on the mirrored wall—are the washbasin and waterspout. ◄

419

An antique terra-cotta bowl was turned into a sink for the exotic zebrawood countertop. Exposed pipes look sleekly sculptural against the dark walls.

420

A fluted wood pedestal is topped with a Carrara marble sink in a mountain-house powder room, pared down to the essence of simplicity.

421

An antique sideboard became a vanity in the powder room of a 1920s house. Blue-and-white porcelain platters hanging on grasscloth-covered walls are an unexpected element in a bathroom, and the chinoiserie-style lantern sconces are a quirky addition.

422

Hugely atmospheric, a rough-cut matte marble basin carved from a single block contrasts with the delicate needlework of the embroidered vintage hand towels. The towel bars are stacked like a ladder, producing a high-spirited and thoroughly original effect.

423

Hand-painted Portuguese tiles and an Indian bone mirror turn a powder room into a little haven of global chic.

424

A stylish powder room is a gift to your guests. A glimpse of an inner space, like this arched alcove, makes the room feel larger; the vertical grid of prints and the antique side chair could make you forget that the alcove is actually a water closet!

425

RIGHT: Paint makes the big statement here, giving a narrow space the depth of sea and sky. A glossy finish catches sunshine or lantern light.

426

FAR RIGHT: In this tribute to luxe modernity, sleek features are adornment enough for lacquered aniline-dyed maple paneling and cabinetworks.

427

FAR LEFT: Space-saving yet stately, the washbasin's pillarlike support is a suitably classical mate for paneled woodwork.

428

LEFT: Reminiscent of an era when indoor plumbing was still a novelty, old-school V-groove wainscoting feels right at home in a traditional ensemble.

429

LEFT: Walls are lime-washed to harmonize with the varied finishes of a marble sink, a bronze backsplash, and an iron mirror frame and sconces.

430

ABOVE LEFT: Symmetrically outlining two sconces to match the ebonized mirror frame creates a triptych wide enough to hold its own above a grand vanity.

431

ABOVE RIGHT: Because a second full bath also serves as the powder room, a mini butler's tray was installed, laden with amenities to delight guests.

432

Clinical ceiling-high white tile
was replaced with fanciful Asian-
themed wallpaper (lampshades
mimic the red parasols) and a
faux-bamboo mirror.

433

RIGHT: An everyday ritual is elevated with a Carrara marble basin. The faucet emerges from a stone-mosaic dado in a spectrum of watery hues.

434

FAR RIGHT: In a subtle variation on the standard shine of chrome and mirror glass, a vanity sheathed in silver leaf evokes boudoir glamour.

435

FAR LEFT: Enchanted forest meets princely bower, thanks to a pairing of woodland wallpaper with an inlaid cabinet converted into a vanity.

436

LEFT: Lively scenes and vivid wallpaper reds, plus an eye-catching crimson shade, distract attention from an awkward space.

437

Rooms under eaves can feel cramped, but the low slope was masked by covering it in an aviary-patterned toile that seems to open up the whole space.

438

Antique Moroccan fretwork panels transform a dark leftover space below a stairway into an alluring Orientalist jewel box.

439

Black-and-white flocked wallpaper inspired a graphic scheme. Perforated Moroccan sconces and a two-tone sink enhance the drama of light and dark.

440

Corner sinks were invented for problem areas like this, where doorways limit usable space. This neat application fits its rustic setting to a tee. ◄

Chapter 9 Best of Bath

275

276

277

278

279

280

281

282

283

284

285

286

290

293

294

"PAYING ATTENTION TO SMALL DETAILS CAN BE TRANSFORMATIVE. A FEW PERSONAL TOUCHES—PLUSH TOWELS, A STYLISH SHOWER CURTAIN, BEAUTIFUL BATH PRODUCTS—WILL TURN ANY BATHROOM INTO A RELAXING SPA."—CHRISTINA MURPHY

441

Inspired by antique **FREESTANDING TUBS**, it has a sculptural elegant presence. Available in five finishes. Mercer Bathtub, urbanarchaeology.com.

442

Give bath time a little extra glow with this metal and glass **LANTERN**. Even without a burning candle, it adds a touch of sparkle to the room. Albany Lantern in polished nickel, arteriorshome.com.

443

Treat your bathroom to a soft, natural patina with these watery blue **HANDMADE TILES**. They have an organic texture that is rich with character. Available in sixteen colors.

444

Hang a pair of these **SCONCES** alongside your mirror and bring some nautical ambience to your bathroom. Hamilton Sconce, waterworks.com.

445

How could this **HAND SPRAYER** not put you in a good mood every time you step into the shower? Comes in other cheerful colors. Rainshower Color Collection, groheamerica.com.

446

Lessen the drudgery of a thankless chore with this whimsically ornate toilet **BRUSH HOLDER**. WC Royale porcelain amphora, colorshome.com.

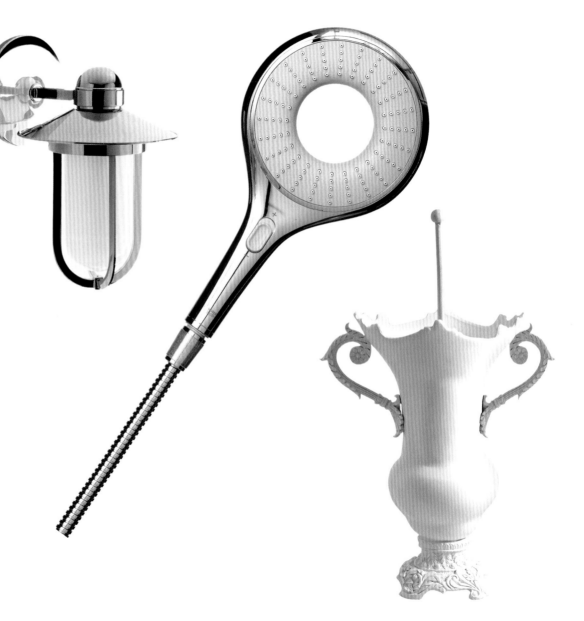

447

This wall-mounted **MIRROR** evokes Palladian windows. And those pivoting side panels are so useful. Inigo mirror, kallista.com.

448

With stylish designs printed on lush Turkish **COTTON TOWELS**, you don't have to settle for solids in your bathroom. Tropical Peacock bath towel, frescotowels.com.

449

A welcome combination of drawers and cabinets! Angled louvers not only give the **VANITY** architectural detail, they provide ventilation. Shutter Double Vanity Sink, restorationhardware.com.

450

This hand-hammered brass **BASIN** celebrates the lotus, long revered in India as a symbol of beauty and perfection. Kamal Lotus Wash Basin, odegardinc. com.

451

With a white glass drum-shaped shade atop a spherical base, this **SCONCE** looks like a classic table lamp for your walls. Bach-style sconce, troy-lighting.com.

452

With its crisp angles and edges, this **TUB** looks dramatic, but you might wonder how it feels. The inside was designed with comfort in mind: sculpted lumbar support, generous depth, and a surface like smooth stone. Askew Freestanding Bath, kohler.com.

453

If **TOWELS** could ever be called happy, these would be the ones. They'll put a smile on your face every morning. Ruffle Bath Towels, echodesign.com.

454

Part **SOAP DISH**, part soap saver—it allows the bar to dry thoroughly, so it lasts longer. Made of recycled bamboo chopsticks. Flat Soap Dish, chopstickart. com.

455

A fluted **FAUCET** that takes inspiration from ancient Greece. Check out those Ionic capitals! Aphrodite Faucet, solid brass in polished-chrome finish, rohlhome. com.

456

Traditional hand-loomed linen **BATH TOWELS** are a great alternative to terrycloth. They're antimicrobial and get better and softer with every wash. Mykolas Linen Towels, anichini.com.

457

This unusual footed **BASKET** makes a handsome home for towels. Pedestal Rectangular Rattan Basket in White Wash, saffrontradingcompany.com.

458

A modern interpretation of the classic bamboo motif, this **SHOWER CURTAIN RING** is perfect for an all-white bathroom.

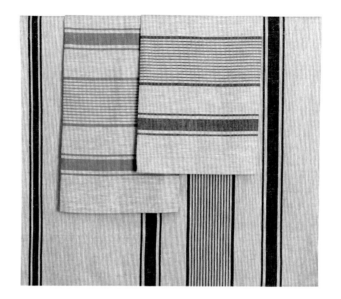

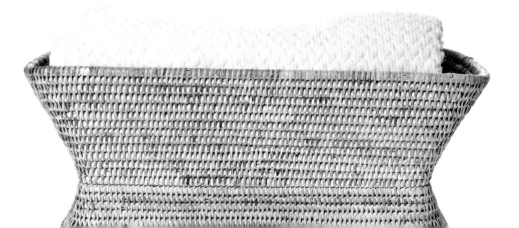

459

Graceful **VESSELS** sculpted out of solid marble, in a range of colors, have mid-century modern roots and can be converted to sinks. Nahbi Bowl Collection, charlesluck.com.

460

Add a chic, graphic touch to your shower floor with this **DRAIN GRID**. Craftsman StyleDrain in Satin Nickel, calfaucets.com.

461

Remarkably lightweight, yet surprisingly absorbent, these two-tone chambray **TOWELS** have two sides: smooth cotton and a looped terrycloth weave. Yoshii Towel, rikumo.com.

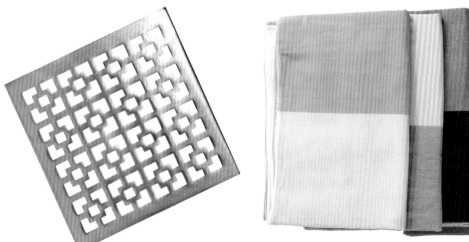

462

A little tubside **TABLE** to hold whatever you need during a long, relaxing soak. Nickel-plated round metal table, mothology.com.

463

In vibrant green, a classic **MOROCCAN TILE** pattern has the look of a formal garden plan. Nejarine tile, mosaichse.com.

464

Usually featured in white, **PENNY TILES** look soft and refreshing in a field of green. Savoy Penny Rounds in Mint, annsacks.com.

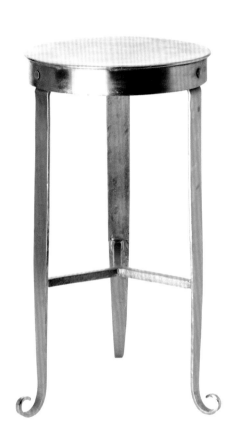

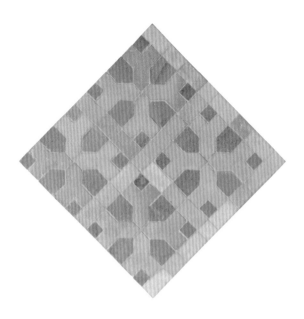

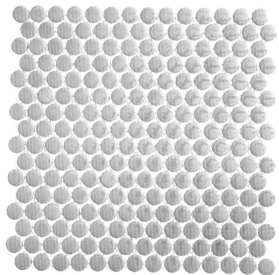

465

Star light, star bright—at 13 ½ inches across, this **LIGHT FIXTURE** is just the right size for a smaller room. Sophia Flush Mount in Natural Brass, circalighting.com.

466

Work the lever on this **SHOWERHEAD** to switch between a soothing drizzle and a robust downpour. WaterSense certified. Isabel Multi-Function Eco-Performance Rainshower, moen.com.

467

Blue, gray, and citrine stripes call to mind the hues of a sun-kissed seascape. A great **VANITY** for those who love the look of a furnished bath. Seaside Vanity, vanitybath.com.

468

A **DRAWER PULL** that will give cabinets a lighter, more modern look. Grafton Pull in Polished Nickel, restorationhardware.com.

469

Handsome abaca rope **STORAGE** for extra hand towels, toilet paper, and other necessities. Yvon Boxes, mecoxgardens.com.

470

The cheerful colors and lively pattern of these **TOWELS** will perk up your bathroom. Multi-colored Turkish towels, inventori.com.

471

Here's a truly sleek matched **CLEANING SET**: waste bin, plunger, and toilet brush. WC Line in Ferrari Red, kontextur.com.

472

Why settle for a **SHOWERHEAD** when you can have a "rain panel?" With three unique sprays: massage, waterfall, or an air-water mix. Raindance Rainfall Air in Chrome, hansgrohe-usa.com.

473

A classic and timeless **PEDESTAL SINK**, with a built-in backsplash for an extra dose of character. Savina Pedestal Lavatory, porcher-us.com.

474

Everything you need for that evening soak, right at your fingertips. **WOODEN BATH RACK**, simplementeblanco.com.

475

The crisp, clean stripes of this rope-wrapped soy **CANDLE** invigorate the room, while the variety of fresh scents lift your spirit. Glass candle, paddywax.com.

476

A wall-mounted **TOILET** (the tank is hidden in the wall) is a great option for a tight space. Aquia Wall-Hung Dual-Flush Toilet, totousa.com.

477

A **VANITY** with demi-lune shape that recalls eighteenth-century France, with curved-front paneling. It can be customized with the paint color of your choice. restorationhardware.com.

478

Really dress up your cabinet doors with a pair of these drop-dead glamorous **PULLS**. Louis XVI Tassel Pull, peguerin.com.

479

COTTON, **ORGANIC TOWELS**, dyed with all-natural ingredients. Japan Polk-Dot Gauze Bath Towels, prairiedog.com.

480

Exotic ikat is beautifully interpreted in jewel **GLASS MOSAIC TILE**. Weft in Quartz and Pearl, newravenna.com.

481

The natural beauty of reclaimed teak of this **STOOL** speaks for itself. The glossy white legs give it a little edge. serenaandlily.com.

482

Soak in it! This **TUB** features hydrotherapy treatments that utilize sound waves, as well as chromatherapy. Underscore Bath with VibrAcoustic Technology, kohler.com.

483

Streamlined style in this sturdy enameled cast iron **TUB**, its standard size and one-piece construction means easy installation. Bellwether Bath, kohler.com.

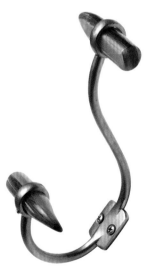

484

A handsome **HOOK** to keep your robe at hand—and your walls looking just so. Antler Melody Hook in iron and horn, anthropologie.com.

485

If you like a warm farmhouse feel, this is the **VANITY** for you. The William Single Sink Console in Pine and Carrara Marble has a white porcelain sink. potterybarn.com.

486

A **FAUCET** that's compact yet commanding, with its upright porcelain-clad levers and a graceful high-neck spout. Rohl Perrin & Rowe Jubilee Collection, rohlhome.com.

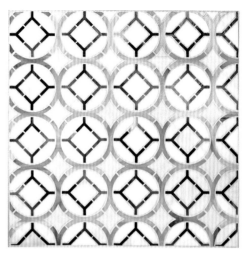

487

Striking **STAINED-GLASS TILES** really dress up a backsplash. Available in thirty colors and eight other patterns. Devotion Series, Cathedral in Era Blend, mandalatile.com.

488

Pick your pattern for a fun update to the usual sinkside **WATER GLASS**. Brighton Tumblers, shopterrain.com.

489

A sleek **HAND MIRROR** that will help you look your best, from all sides! Looks good on your vanity, too. Mirror Mirror, dwr.com.

490

Pendleton brings its historic Native American blanket patterns to **BATH TOWELS**. This 1920s design celebrates Chief Joseph, legendary leader of the Nez Perce. pendleton-usa.com.

491

A striking **VANITY** design that takes inspiration from the chrome-plated grilles of vintage luxury cars. Wide Blues Console (includes ceramic mono-block double basin), devon-devon.com.

492

Mopping the bathroom is no one's favorite chore. Let this little **ROBOT** do the work! At less than seven inches in diameter, it gets into tight spaces. Scooba, irobot.com.

493

Bold stripes in handwoven cotton **TOWELS** add a lively color punch. They're big enough to use as beach towels, for picnics, and on tabletops! Mighty Stripe Towels, karaweaves.com.

494

It has the grand look of a freestanding cast-iron **TUB**, but in lightweight acrylic, so it's really easy to install. Also available as an air bath. Parisian 2, mtibaths.com.

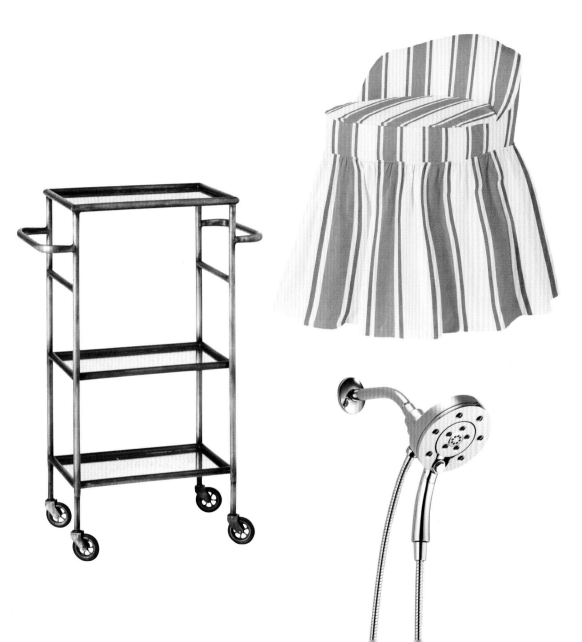

495

This versatile **CART** could go anywhere, but with its mirrored shelves and towel bars, it's just right for the bath. Iron and Mirror Cart, rejuvenation.com.

496

Available in a range of fabrics, colors, and patterns, so you can really make this **STOOL** your own. Upholstered Swivel Stool, ballarddesigns.com.

497

No need to choose between wall-mounted and handheld **SPRAYERS**—you can have both! The hand unit docks magnetically when not in use. Odin Hydrati Two-in-One Shower, brizo.com.

498

A **DIFFUSER** with the beauty of a perfume bottle. Invert it like an hourglass bottle to infuse the room with its delicate fragrance. 34 Boulevard Saint Germain Diffuser, diptyqueparis.com.

499

A versatile **PULL** for cabinetry that works in a modern or traditional space. Small Satin Brass Ring Pull (also available in Polished or Satin Nickel), lahardware.com.

500

The six-foot mirrored **CABINET** door hides a jumbo storage space. Mount it on, or set it into, a wall. Frame Metal Full-Length Medicine Cabinet, restorationhardware.com.

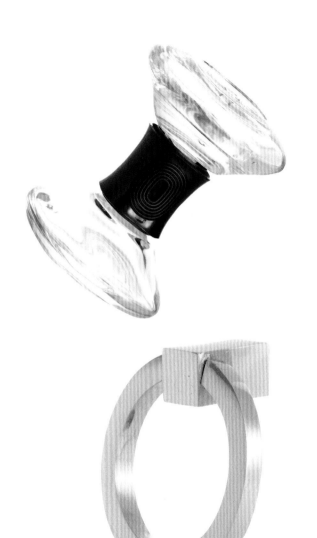

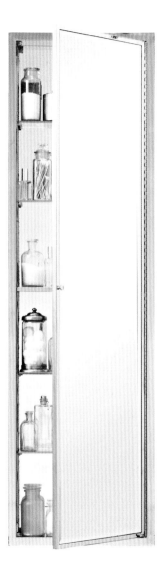

Photo Credits

Front Cover: Lisa Romerein
Back Cover (clockwise from top): Roger Davies, Jonny Valiant, Victoria Pearson

Edward Addeo: 77 top left, 79, 80 (both)
Lucas Allen: 52, 53 (both), 94, 95 (both)
Quentin Bacon: 77 top row (second from right), 77 top right, 83, 84, 85 (both), 201 left
Christopher Baker: 13 bottom row (second from right), 70, 110, 161 middle row (second from right), 173, 211 bottom right, 241 right
Chuck Baker: 192 right
John Bessler: 20, 77 top center, 82, 153, 156, 170 left, 255 right, 266 top right, 269 bottom left
Antoine Bootz: 101 middle right, 119
James Carrière: 133 bottom right, 158, 159 (all photos), 187 top right, 187 middle left, 193, 194
Jonn Coolidge: 267 middle
Roger Davies: 101 top center, 107 left, 211 top right, 221
Reed Davis: 132, 133 bottom left, 149 (both), 187 top left, 187 top row (second from left), 189, 190 (both), 216 left, 243 middle row (second from left), 256 right
François Dischinger: 101 bottom row (second from right), 128, 129 left
Jason Donnelly: 13 bottom (second from left), 60, 61, 62, 63
Miki Duisterhof: 161 bottom (second from left), 161 bottom center, 179 (both), 180
Pieter Estersohn: 13 middle row (second from right), 54 (both), 55, 101 top right, 112, 151 right, 152, 161 middle row center, 169, 172 right, 182 right, 210, 239, 242, 250 left, 252, 266 top left, 269 top right
Don Freeman: 16, 46, 47, 74, 157 left, 175 right, 199, 201 right, 243 bottom left, 257 right, 260, 264, 266 bottom right
J. Savage Gibson: 27
Susan Gilmore: 101 bottom center, 127

Tria Giovan: 234
John Granen: 13 top center, 31, 32-33 (all photos)
Gridley + Graves: 100, 113, 114
Mick Hales: 211 top center, 216 right
John M. Hall: 150 left
Ken Hayden: 243 middle left, 255 left, 256 left
Heddenphillips.com: 13 bottom left, 58, 59, 126 right, 272
Alec Hemer: 224 (both)
Ditte Isager: 228 right
John Kernick: 76, 77 middle left, 77 middle row (second from left), 86, 87 (both), 88 (both), 187 bottom row (second from left), 202, 267 top
Francesco Lagnese: 13 top row (second from right), 28 (both), 37 left, 38 right, 40, 41, 77 bottom row (second from right), 97, 101 top row (second from right), 101 middle left, 101 bottom right, 109, 115 right, 131, 161 middle row (second from left), 171 right, 186, 187 middle center, 196 left, 203, 211 middle row (second from right), 229 (both), 243 middle right, 243 bottom row (second from right), 243 bottom right, 263, 268, 270 left, 271 left
Michael J. Lee: 217, 218 left
David Duncan Livingston: 67 right
Thomas Loof: 42 left, 43, 67 left, 111 left, 133 top right, 133 middle right, 142 (both), 148 (both), 187 middle row (second from right), 197 (all photos), 207, 208, 211 middle center, 211 bottom (second from right), 220, 223, 226, 238, 243 middle center, 254 left, 259 left
Peter Margonelli: 133 middle center, 133 middle row (second from right), 145, 146
Sylvia Martin: 211 top left, 213
Kerri McCaffety: 195 right, 259 right
Maura McEvoy: 174 left
James Merrell: 13 top right, 13 bottom center, 42 right, 45, 64, 65, 66 (all photos), 115 left, 161 top center, 166 (both), 214, 243 top row (second from left), 246 left, 251, 257 left

Karyn R. Millet: 8, 13 top row (second from left), 25, 26, 187 middle right, 187 bottom right, 198, 209, 211 top row (second from left), 215 (both), 247 right
Matthew Millman: 2, 13 middle center, 50, 51 (both)
Laura Moss: 269 top left
Ngoc Minh Ngo: 13 middle right, 56, 57 (all photos), 72 left, 96 left, 106, 107 right, 125 right, 161 top left, 161 top row (second from left), 161 middle right, 163, 164, 165 (both), 175 left, 211 top row (second from right), 219 right, 243 top row (second from right), 250 right
Amy Neunsinger: 73, 101 bottom left, 111 right, 120, 129 right, 172 left, 176 left, 187 top row (second from right), 192 left, 204 left, 211 bottom left, 233 (both), 243 bottom row (second from left), 247 middle, 265 left
Victoria Pearson: 13 top left, 17, 18, 37 right, 39 (both), 77 middle center, 77 middle row (second from right), 77 middle right, 77 bottom left, 77 bottom row (second from left), 89, 90, 91 (both), 92 (all photos), 93 (all photos), 98, 101 middle row (second from left), 101 bottom row (second from left), 116 left, 121, 174 right, 182 left, 187 bottom left, 187 bottom center, 187 bottom row (second from right), 200, 204 right, 206, 211 middle right, 253 right, 225 right, 230 right, 232, 235 left, 239 right, 243 top right, 243 bottom center, 253 right, 267 left
Eric Piasecki: 15, 72 right, 77 bottom center, 96 right, 122, 150 right, 161 top row (second from right), 167, 187 top center, 191 left, 253 left, 258, 262, 265 right
Michael Price: 101 middle row center, 117 right
David Prince: 133 bottom row (second from right), 157 right
Paul Raeside: 117 left
Laura Resen: 219 left

Designer Credits

Dana Abbot & Kim Fiscus: 187 top row (2nd from right), 192 left

Alla Akimova: 133 top (2nd from right); 139-141

Pierce Allen: 52-53

Butler Armsden Architecture & Angela Free Design: 133 bottom right, 158-159

Christopher Baker: 161 middle (2nd from right), 173

Ginger Barber: 211 middle right, 230 right

Diamond Barrata: 101 middle right, 119

Chris Barrett for KAA Design Group: 225 right

Healing Barsanti: 77 top middle, 82

Ruby Beets Old & New: 201 right

Robin Bell: 46, 47, 266 bottom right

Barrie Benson: 123-124, 125 left

Jonathan Berger: 101 middle left

Mona Ross Berman: Back cover bottom right, 243 top left, 245

Penelope Bianchi: 187 bottom row center, 204 right

Jeffrey Bilhuber: 74, 157 left, 187 middle row (2nd from right), 197, 243 bottom left, 264

Kyle Timothy Blood: 13 middle row (2nd from left), 48, 49

Laura Bohn: 77 top, 84, 83, 85

Bonesteel & Trout: Back Cover bottom left, 8, 77, 89-93, 211 top row (2nd from left), 215

Nancy Bozhardt: 28, 267 top right

Meg Braff: 115 left, 214, 251, 269 bottom right

Annie Brahler: 130

Alessandra Branca: 170 left

Brockschmidt & Coleman: 75 right

Betsy Brown: 175 right, 257 right

Betsy Burnham: 73, 247 middle

Liza Pulitzer Calhoun: 186, 203, 243 middle row right, 263

Thomas Catalano and Chris Benson: 101 top left, 101 top (2nd from left), 103-105

Eric Cohler: 108 left

Kim Coleman & Michele Green: 45, 257 left

Nancy Corzine: 256 left

Robert Couturier: 243 top row (2nd from left), 246 left

Eleanor Cummings: 187 top middle, 191 left, 258

Kari Cusack: 13 top row (2nd from left), 25-26, 247 right

Frank Delledonne: 37 left

Kerry Delrose: 150 left

Kim Dempster & Erin Martin: 224

Orlando Diaz-Azcuy: 67 right

Barry Dixon: 69, 68, 77 top left, 79-80

T. Keller Donovan: 101 center, 117 right, 243 middle left, 255 left

Kay Douglass: 231

Peter Dunham: 98, 187 bottom row (2nd from right), 206

Douglas Durkin and Greg Elich: 72 right

David Easton: 153, 156, 266 top right

Karin Edwards: 13 bottom (2nd from left), 60-63

Emily Evans Eerdman: 161 top right, 168, 243 top row center, 249 right

Mark Egerstrom: 240

Chad Eisner: 187 middle row right, 198

Krista Ewart: 101 middle row (2nd from left), 116 left

Waldo Fernandez: 234

Susan Ferrier of McAlpine Booth & Ferrier Interiors: 13 bottom (2nd from right), 70, 133 top right, 142 left

Susan Ferrier, design; Bobby McAlpine, McAlpine Tanksersly, architect: 16, 150 right, 260

Thom Filicia: 111 left

Kirsten Fitzgibbons & Kelli Ford: 13 top right, 42 right

Andrew Flesher: 101 bottom middle, 127

Form Architecture + Interiors: 151 right, 152, 210, 239, 250 left

Ken Fulk: 2, 13 center, 50-51, 101 bottom right, 107 right, 125 right, 131, 187 bottom right, 187 bottom left, 200, 209, 237 right

Fawn Galli: 249 left

Steven Gambrel: 122, 205 left, 246 right

Kelie Grosso: 96 left, 106, 243 top row, 250 right

Andrew Halliday & David Greer: 142 right

Lindsey Coral Harper: 161 middle right, 175 left

Carrie Hayden: 13 top row (middle), 31-33

Deirdre Heekin & Caleb Barber: 228 right

Bernt Heiberg & William Cummings: 161 middle left, 170 right

Kristin Hein & Philip Cozzi: 133 bottom (2nd from left), 151 left

Shawn Henderson: 133, 143-144, 201 left

Emily Henry: 216 left

Lorraine Herr & Randall Netley: 13 middle row (far right), 56-57

Amy Aidinis Hirsch: 94-95

Myra Hoefer: 38 right, 182 left

Martin Horner: 13 top row (2nd from rt), 40-41

Phoebe Howard: 27, 269 top left

James Michael Howard: 77 bottom (2nd from right), 97

Bill Ingram: 181, 211 top left, 213, 241 left

Tracery Interiors: 13 bottom right, 75 left

Kathryn M. Ireland: 174 right

Jay Jeffers: 187, 193-194

Noel Jeffrey: 43

Chipper Joseph, design; Glenn Arbonies & Sandra Vlock, Arbonies King Vlock, architecture: 174 left

Susan Noble Jones: 161 top middle, 166

Nickey Kehoe: 204 left, 235 left

Laura Kirar: 6, 21-24, 270 right

Todd Klein: 248

David Kleinberg: 110, 242, 252

Leslie Klotz: 219 left

John Knott & John Fondas: 171 left

Carol Kurth: 133 top (2nd from left), 133 top middle, 137-138

Jean Larette: 132, 133 bottom left, 149

Adam Leskinen, Bjørnen Design: 161 top left, 161 top (2nd from left), 163-165

Richard H. Lewis: 161 bottom (2nd from right), 183

Zim Loy: 108 right, 243 middle row (2nd from right), 261 right

Sarah Luhtala, design; David Katz, architecture: 133 top left, 135-136
Peter Mark & Elizabeth Needham: 161 bottom left, 176-178
Sally Markham: 169, 266 top left, 269 top right
Erin Martin: 191 right, 225 left
Gary McBournie: 254 right
Brian McCarthy: 187 center, 196 left
Mary McDonald: 38 left
Kelley McDowell: 101 bottom (2nd from left), 121
Mimi Maddock McMakin: 211 middle row (second from right), 229, 243 bottom right, 271 left
Maine Design: 39, 243 top right, 253 right
Gideon Mendelson: 77 bottom center, 96 right
Will Merrill: 230 left
Anne Miller: 265 right
Jill Morris: 192 right
Heather Moore & Jed Johnson Associates: 133 middle right, 148
Paolo Moschino: 19, 205 right
Christina Murphy: 211 top row (2nd from right), 219 right
Joe Nahem: Back Cover top, 211 top right, 221, 254 left
David Netto: 187 middle row (2nd from left), 195 left, 228 left
Amy Neunsinger: 101 bottom left, 120, 172 left
Joe Nye: 101 middle (2nd from right), 101 top middle, 107 left, 118, 267 middle
Marie Nygren & Smith Hanes: 176 left
Ellen O'Neill: 187 bottom row (2nd from left), 202
Allison Paladino: 253 left
Jennifer Palumbo: 217-218
Alex Papachristidis: 42 left
Karyl Pierce Paxton: 195 right
Victoria Pearson: 232
Betty Lou Phillips: 12, 35-36
Royce Pinkwater: 211 center, 226
Melanie Pounds: 211 bottom row (2nd from right), 238
J. Randall Powers: 71
Miles Redd: 67 left
Amanda Reilly: 29-30
Michael Richman: 76-77, 86-88

Kathleen Rivers, design; Stanley Dixon, architect: 101 top (2nd from right), 109
Lawrence Rizkowski: 187 top left, 187 top row (2nd from left), 189-190, 243 middle row (2nd from left), 256 right
Markham Roberts: 211 bottom right, 241 right
Frank Roop: 161 middle (2nd from left), 171 right
Dan Ruhland: 13 bottom center, 64-66
John Saladino: 15
Franklin Salasky: 182 right
Barbara Sallick (Waterworks): 161 bottom middle, 161 bottom (2nd from left), 179-180
Tom Samet & Ross Meltzer: 117 left
Fern Santini: 72 left
Sara Scaglione: 126 left
Steven Scarloff: 101 bottom (2nd from right), 128, 129 left
Tom Scheerer: 196 right, 270 left
Charles O. Schwarz III: 211 top row center, 216 right
Kathryn Scott: 133 bottom (2nd from right), 157 right
SCW Interiors: 100, 113-114
Jacqueline Derry Segura: 77 bottom right, 99
Pamela Shamshiri for Commune.: 211 bottom left, 233
Stephen Shubel: 13 middle row (far left), 44, 77 top 2nd from left, 81, 271 right
Mark D. Sikes & Michael Griffin: 111 right, 129 right, 243 bottom row (2nd from left), 265 left
Paul Siskin: 13 middle row (2nd from right), 54-55
Cindy Smith, design; Ken Pursley, architect: 20, 255 right
Windsor Smith: 13 top left, 17-18, 37 right
Michael S. Smith: Front Cover, 208, 211 middle left, 222, 243 center, 247 left, 259 left, 266 bottom left
Robert Stilin, design; Frank Greenwald, architect: 227
Madeline Stuart: 243 bottom center, 267 left
Lee Ann Thornton: 220
Carleton Varney: 116 right
Ruard Veltman: 161 top (2nd from right), 167, 262
Babs Watkins, Julie Watkins Baker, Eleanor Cummings: 259 right
Barbara Westbrook: 101 top right, 112, 161 center, 172 right
Jack Wettling: 10-11, 161 bottom right, 184-185

Jeannette Whitson: 261 left
Ashley Whittaker: 243 bottom row (2nd from right), 268
Bunny Williams: 223
Vicente Wolf: 5, 133 bottom middle, 154-155
Mary Watkins Wood: 207

Index